D1254689

Art and Architecture

Inside ANCIENT GREECE

Art *and* Architecture

ANNE WRIGHT

Sharpe Focus

an imprint of M.E. Sharpe, Inc.

First edition for the United States, its territories and dependencies,
Canada, Mexico, and Australia, published in 2008 by M.E. Sharpe, Inc.

Sharpe Focus
An imprint of M.E. Sharpe, Inc.
80 Business Park Drive
Armonk, NY 10504

www.mesharpe.com

Library of Congress Cataloging-in-Publication Data

Wright, Anne Margaret.
  Art and architecture / Anne Wright.
     p. cm. -- (Inside ancient Greece)
  Includes bibliographical references and index.
  ISBN 978-0-7656-8130-0 (hardcover : alk. paper)
  1. Art, Greek--Juvenile literature. 2. Art, Ancient--Greece--Juvenile
literature. 3. Architecture, Ancient--Greece--Juvenile literature. I.
Title.

N5630.W75 2008
709.38--dc22

                          2007011418

Editorial and design by Amber Books Ltd
Project Editor: James Bennett
Copy Editor: Deborah Murrell
Picture Research: Kate Green
Design: Andrew Easton

Cover Design: Jesse Sanchez, M.E. Sharpe, Inc.

Printed in Malaysia

9 8 7 6 5 4 3 2 1

For Gavin Hannah, FSA,
do tibi mille basia, deinde centum…

PICTURE CREDITS
AKG-Images: 6–7, 8, 10, 11, 24, 25, 31, 32, 33, 34, 38, 39, 44, 49, 50, 54, 55, 56–57, 58, 60, 61, 72,
73 (all), 74
Corbis: 16, 21
De Agostini: 12, 14, 15, 17, 18–19, 22, 27, 29, 35, 36, 37, 42, 45, 46, 47, 48, 52, 56, 62, 63, 65, 67,
68, 70–71

ABOUT THE AUTHOR
Anne Wright gained a First Class Honours degree from the University of St. Andrews, Scotland,
before moving on to further study at Corpus Christi College, University of Oxford. After teaching in
London, she moved back to Oxford, where she is currently Head of Classics at Summer Fields, an
independent boys' boarding school. She lives in Oxford, U.K.

Contents

Introduction

The civilization of the ancient Greeks has influenced the world for thousands of years. Much of what we take for granted today, in areas such as science, mathematics, drama, poetry, and philosophy, was invented by the ancient Greeks. In many other fields, too, the Greeks made huge advances in human knowledge. Modern politicians still look for inspiration to fifth-century B.C.E. Athens, the cradle of democracy. Ancient Greek plays are still performed today, and in all the major cities of the world you can find buildings heavily influenced by Greek architecture. This series of books explores the full richness of Greek culture and history. It also considers how Greek civilization still influences us today.

Art and Architecture

When we think about Greek art, we often visualize creamy-white polished marble statues. However, Greek artists did not at first create this type of statue. Sculptors experimented with a variety of styles before they finally arrived at the classical model. Experiments with bronze also had a great influence on those sculptors who worked in stone. As a result, to this day we can still see many of the great statues in both bronze and stone.

While many statues were often made for public display, the most common form of Greek art was the painted vase. Thousands of pottery vases have survived from the Greek world, and many preserve fine examples of painted scenes from both mythology and everyday life.

As well as exploring sculpture and pottery, this book also considers painting and other art forms, such as jewelry and coinage. Changes in Greek art are also discussed, together with the extent to which these developments influenced later artists and sculptors.

This artist's impression shows a procession entering the Acropolis at Athens, the site of some of the Greek world's most spectacular temples.

In addition, *Art and Architecture* describes the many kinds of different building which the Greeks constructed, such as houses, meeting places, and theaters. However, the most important buildings in a Greek town or city were the temples. Temples were the homes of the gods and were intended to be as large and splendid as possible. These temples were often decorated with sculptures that were painted in bright colors. The final chapter explains how temples were built and discusses the detail to be found on different temples.

Chapter One

Vase Painting

Art was very important to the ancient Greeks. They surrounded themselves with a wide range of beautiful things, including jewelry, painting, sculpture, and mosaics. These art forms were often made from expensive materials, such as gold, silver, bronze, or marble. However, one of the most popular and common forms of Greek art was vase painting, to be found on the humble clay pot. Although clay is not an expensive material, pottery vases preserve some of the finest examples of Greek painting to survive from the ancient Greek world.

Pottery had a wide variety of uses in the ancient world, ranging from roof tiles to perfume bottles. Every Greek household had many different pieces of pottery. Much of this pottery consisted of plain, unadorned objects to be used in the kitchen. However, there were also highly decorated vases, such as drinking cups or large storage jars given as prizes at athletic contests. These decorated vases preserve examples of some of the finest art produced in the Greek world, and they survive in very large numbers—there are thousands and thousands of pots exhibited in the world's museums. As well as being beautiful, Greek pots often convey an enormous amount of information about everyday life. Pots show everything from women preparing for a wedding to children at school and men harvesting olives.

This Corinthian amphora shows the death of a centaur. A variety of stylized birds are painted around the top of the vase and on the handles.

How Were Pots Made?

The basic ingredient of a pot is clay. Clay would have been kneaded, as it is today, to get rid of any air pockets, and then shaped into a pot. Some of the earliest Greek pots were shaped by hand, but pottery techniques greatly improved after the introduction of a flat rotating disk, known as a wheel. When a wheel was used, a ball of clay was put on top of the disk and one potter molded the clay as it rotated, while the wheel was turned by a second potter (often an apprentice learning the trade). The rotating action of the wheel enabled the curves of the pot to be even on all sides, rather than lopsided. After the basic shape was made, the pot would be painted. Handles were fixed onto the pot and the completed object baked in a kiln.

Why Does Pottery Survive?

When archaeologists excavate sites from the ancient world, the single most common item they find is pottery. This is because clay pots, although they break fairly easily, are very difficult to destroy entirely. People do not attempt to reuse broken pots, so they tend to lie in the ground, waiting to be discovered and pieced back together. Sometimes pots filled with oil or food were buried in graves and these may survive intact, hidden under the earth. Other forms of art do not survive as easily. Gold jewelry and bronze statues can be melted down and the valuable metal reused. Marble statues can be crushed up for lime, and wall paintings are destroyed when buildings collapse.

Color Changes

Pottery has to be fired in a kiln to make it strong and capable of holding water. Firing means exposing the pot to intense heat (around 1700° F, or 950° C) inside the kiln. Owing to the temperature, a chemical reaction takes place in the clay and the grayish color of unfired clay changes. Most clay contains iron, and this causes it to develop into a rich terra-cotta color when fired. The clay from Attica (the region around Athens) was particularly rich in iron, and was prized for its warm orange-red terra-cotta color. However, the clay found in the region of Corinth turned into a yellow-brown color. Many

of the pots in museums today that have a yellowish background color were made in Corinth. Decoration was applied by using a shiny black slip (or thin glaze of clay). Most pots were terra-cotta and black, but sometimes white or a darker red slip was also used.

This vase shows two formations of warriors marching into battle. Different colored paint has been used to show the skin tones and the patterns on the shields.

Shapes

The ancient Greeks used pots in a variety of ways, and the shapes of the pots reflected their different purposes. For example, Greeks did not have running water, but had to fetch it from a spring or fountain. A *hydria* (*HOO-dree-ah*), or water pot, would need to be large and easy to carry, whereas a perfume bottle would be small and would not need handles.

Large pots were used for storage. As well as water jars, there were *amphoras* (*am-forr-ah*) and *kraters* (*KRAH-ter*). Amphoras were used to store wine, olive oil, and sometimes dry goods, such as grain. They had a wide body with a narrow neck and had two handles. Some amphoras were specially painted with scenes showing athletic competitions. These were filled with olive oil and awarded as prizes at various festivals. Such vases would have been a source of great pride in the home of the victor. Kraters were used to mix wine and water together. A jug called an *oinochoe* (*oi-no-KO-ay*) would have been used to serve the wine into smaller cups called *skyphoi* (*SKIFF-oi*). As well as the *skyphos* (*SKIFF-oss*), there were two other types of drinking cups. A *kylix* (*KI-lix*), had a shallow flat base whereas a *kantharos* (*KAN-tha-ross*) looked like a mug, with two large, curly handles.

Small pots were also used for storage. A *pyxis* (*PICK-sis*) was a small circular box with a lid and was used to keep various items of makeup. Perfume or ointments would be kept in an *alabastron* (*ala-BAS-tron*) or an *aryballos* (*arr-EE-ball-oss*). An alabastron was a tall, thin bottle, which usually had a white background, whereas an aryballos was a small, squat jar and was usually decorated with black and terra-cotta.

A *lekythos* was a small vase that was often buried in graves.

Why Was Olive Oil So Important?

The ancient Greeks cooked with olive oil, as we do today, but they also used it for cleaning and lighting. The Greeks did not have electricity or gas supplies to light their homes, but instead burned olive oil in an oil lamp. When olive oil was refined and had perfume added to it, it could be used as a type of soap for cleaning. There was therefore a great demand for olive oil throughout the Greek world. This demand was very useful to the Athenians. The soil of Athens is not good for growing ordinary crops, but it does produce very good olive trees. Athenians could therefore harvest the olives, produce the oil, and then export it. The money that the oil brought in enabled the Athenians to buy large amounts of grain, which they could not produce easily on their own land. Naturally, the olive oil had to be exported in containers. The growing trade in oil meant that there was a need for many pots, and Athens became one of the leading manufacturers of pottery. Indeed, there was a whole area in Athens devoted to pottery workshops, known as the Kerameikos (*ker-ah-MAY-ee-koss*), or Area of the Potters. (The English word "ceramic" comes from the Greek word "*keramikos*," [*ke-RAM-i-koss*] which means something made of clay.)

Vases for Special Occasions

Although pots were often used daily, there were some types of pots that were kept for special occasions, such as the amphoras that were awarded as prizes in athletic contests. When children reached the age of three or four, they took part in a festival called the Choes (*KO-ays*) or the "festival of the jugs." This festival was held to mark the fact that

Amphoras were large storage vessels and were often highly decorated. This amphora was painted around 540–530 B.C.E. and shows Achilles killing the Amazon Queen Penthesilea.

children had passed babyhood and had their first taste of wine. To commemorate the occasion, children were given a small wine jug called a *chous* (*hoos*). If a child died young, these vases were often buried in their grave. The death of adults would also require pottery. Vases containing food or perfume were often buried in the grave, and sometimes large vases were placed to mark the grave. There was even a specific type of pot associated with burials. This was called a *lekythos* (*leck-EE-thoss*) and it was usually made out of whitish clay and painted with pictures of mourners.

The happier side of life was also celebrated with pots. The night before her marriage, a bride had a special bath. The water was brought from a sacred spring in a *loutrophoros* (*LOO-tro-FOUR-oss*) vase. This tall vase with long handles was often decorated with scenes of wedding preparations or other aspects of a woman's life.

Patterns and Pictures

The decoration on Greek pottery changed considerably over time. It is not always possible to date exactly when a pot was made, and archaeologists often refer to pots as having been made at some point over a ten-, twenty-, or even fifty-year period. The very earliest decorated Greek pots come from Crete around the fifteenth century B.C.E. The island situation of Crete clearly influenced some of the painters of these pots, which often have sea scenes portrayed on them. Stylized drawings of octopus or fish were particularly popular. Flowers and other plants were also common. By the fourteenth century B.C.E., the mainland Greeks were producing large pots with pictures of humans, such as men driving a chariot.

After the Late Bronze Age of the fifteenth to thirteenth centuries B.C.E., Greece fell into the Dark Ages. There is little material evidence from this period and it is only in the eleventh century B.C.E. that archaeologists can start to identify a new style called Protogeometric. Protogeometric pots were decorated with a variety of lines. Often these were just simple bands around the outside of the pot, but sometimes there was a series of circles or half-circles. Further development of this type of decoration led to the Geometric style.

The Geometric Style

One of the best examples of the Geometric style is the Dipylon (*DIP-i-lon*) Vase. This large vase was used to mark a grave, and is split into different sections by painted lines, which wrap around the pot. Within the sets of lines there are different bands of decoration. Near the top and bottom of both the neck and body of the pot, the bands of decoration are much smaller. However, the painter emphasized both the center of the neck and the center of the pot by leaving a wider section for decoration. Some areas have simple geometric patterns, such as triangles or the "Greek Key" pattern. Others show stylized pictures of deer and goats grazing. The main image, however, is of lines of people burying a dead woman. She lies in the center of

Pots—When and What?

The six most important styles of vase painting were spread out over many centuries.

Style	Century B.C.E.	Decoration
Bronze Age	15th to 13th	plants and sea creatures
Protogeometric	11th to 10th	bands of lines or circles
Geometric	9th to 8th	geometric shapes and early representations of people and animals
Orientalizing	late 8th to 7th	stylized animals and plants
Black-figure	early 7th to mid 5th	mythological scenes and everyday life; black figures on a red background
Red-figure	late 6th to end 4th	mythological scenes and everyday life; red figures on a black background

This vase shows a line of marching warriors and was made in the early twelfth century B.C.E.

the scene, surrounded by mourning adults. Most of them are standing, but two sit on stools and two are kneeling in front of the corpse. A single child is represented as a much smaller figure on the right-hand side of the body.

This kind of picture can be found on other Greek vases of a similar period. Pots used to mark the graves of dead men often showed processions of chariots or horses. However, at this early stage of the development of Greek pottery, human figures still lack detail and it is not possible to do much more than show a simple scene.

Orientalizing Pottery

A new style of pottery arose in the late eighth century B.C.E. This was called the Orientalizing style (also known as Proto-Corinthian and Corinthian). By this time, the Greeks had considerable trade links with the East and had been exposed to different artistic styles, many of which showed animals. This exposure influenced how the Greeks painted their own pottery, and they developed a new style with much more detailed paintings of animals and, sometimes, humans.

This new style of pottery (such as the vase on page 8) had brown figures painted on a creamy

This large amphora, called the Dipylon Vase, is over 5 feet (1.5 meters) tall and was used as a grave marker. It was painted around 750 B.C.E. and shows a funeral procession carrying the body of the dead woman.

Owls were very popular on drinking cups. Owls were the symbol of wisdom and were connected with the goddess Athena.

yellow background. Much of the pottery came from Corinth, which was noted for its high-quality pots. Sometimes pottery made outside Corinth was given a yellowish wash to make it look as if it had been made in Corinth. Orientalizing pottery still used lines to break up the pot into various different sections of decoration. Often there would be triangular shapes coming up from the base to emphasize the rounded shape, and the top of the vase usually had a dark band of paint to mark off the end of the decoration.

The main decoration was often split into three central areas, each filled with a row of animals following around the side of the pot. A wide variety of animals appear on these pots: lions, leopards, bulls, deer, goats, wild boars, hunting dogs, and hares were all popular. The vases were made to appear lively by the careful positioning of the animals. Often each row of animals would face in a different direction from the row below it. Stylized plants were used as decoration in between the animals.

Master Painters

Archaeologists date vases first according to what type they are (for example, Geometric or black-figure). Then they group the vases according to various styles within the general type. Sometimes, the style of various vases can be so similar that the same painter must have made them. However, occasionally the painters of vases signed their work. When this happens, we know for certain that they were painted by the same man. For example, one of the finest Greek vase painters was called Exekias (*Ex-EE-kee-as*). He painted both the vase showing Ajax and Achilles playing dice and the vase showing the death of Penthesilea (*Pen-thess-ill-AY-uh*).

This black-figure amphora was painted around 540–530 B.C.E. It shows the heroes Achilles and Ajax playing dice. The painter has tried very hard to show all the details of the warriors' armor.

Black-Figure Pottery

Although Corinth dominated the market for pottery in the eighth and seventh centuries B.C.E., by the end of the sixth century B.C.E., Athens was the major producer of pots. Part of the reason for this change was the introduction of a new style called "black-figure" pottery. Here, black figures were painted on a terra-cotta background. Advances in painting technique meant that people were no longer shown as silhouettes, as they had been in the Geometric style, but in considerable detail. It was now possible to portray actions and events on vases and the Athenian vase painters took full advantage of this development.

Red-Figure Pottery

Red-figure pottery started to be produced from around 530 B.C.E. Instead of having black figures on a red background, red

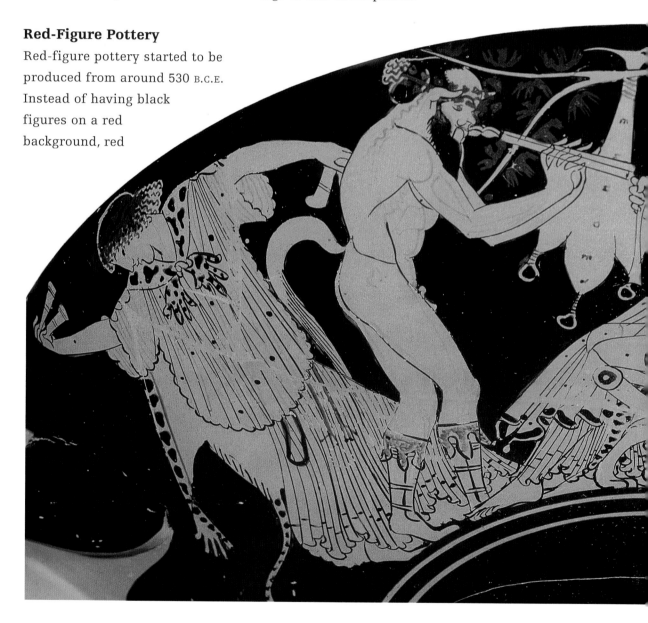

figures were shown on a black background. However, while black-figure pottery was created by painting a black slip (or thin clay) onto the clay background, red-figure pottery was more complicated to create. The red figure was the color of the original clay and the black slip was painted across the entire background, except where the decoration was to show up. The great benefit of this technique was that very thin lines could now be painted onto the figures themselves. This meant that more detail could be shown, particularly when painting facial expressions and clothes.

The picture below illustrates the importance of being able to portray clothes convincingly. The women are wearing leopard skins on top of their robes and it is possible to see how the furs are tied around the women's necks. The folds of the robes ripple and flow, following the shape of the women's bodies as

The outside of this red-figure kylix, or drinking cup, shows women celebrating the arrival of the god Dionysus, who sits while a satyr plays a flute.

they dance. All of these delicate lines help to convey a real sense of movement. Moreover, despite the fact that only two colors are used in this cup, there is no lack of action in this scene.

The Influence of Mythology

Ancient Greeks were fascinated by the tales and legends which had been passed down through the generations. On the earliest examples of Greek pottery, it is impossible to tell whether specific aspects of a myth are being shown. For example, a drawing of a burial scene might have represented the fate of a hero from the Trojan War. Alternatively, such an image could simply have shown a normal funeral. However, as the ability to portray people in greater detail improved, vase painters clearly began to experiment with scenes from mythology. Sometimes the figures would be named, but often the scene would be so clearly drawn that anyone knowing the stories would immediately be able to identify what was happening. Pictures of the adventures of Heracles seem to have been particularly popular, but all the major stories from Greek mythology were regularly represented.

Imported Art

Much of the pottery that has survived from the ancient world was found in Italy or Sicily. This region had been colonized by Greeks from mainland Greece and was known as "Great Greece." Most of the early pots were imported directly from Greece, but from the second half of the fifth century, local potters began to make and paint pots in the style of the imported Athenian vases. Scientific analysis of the clay used in pots can help archaeologists to find out where a particular pot was made.

Later Pottery

By the fourth century B.C.E., Greek painters had begun to experiment with more colors on their pots. Gold, yellow, white, and a deeper red were being used frequently. While this added to the colorfulness of the vase, some of the original delicacy and freshness of the black and red vases were lost. In the third century B.C.E., potters started to produce molded pottery. It appears that this new style was an attempt to imitate vessels made out of metals, such as silver or gold. Molded pottery was made by pressing clay into a mold, removing the mold, and firing the clay. This technique was adapted by the Romans and used to produce red Arretine (*ARR-eh-tine*) ware, which was exported all over the Roman Empire.

15th to 13th	11th to 10th	9th to 8th
Bronze Age	**Protogeometric**	**Geometric**
Formation of Warriors (p.14) early 12th century		

Sleep and Death carry off the body of the hero Sarpedon. Hermes (wearing a hat and winged boots) supervises proceedings. This large pot was painted around 510 B.C.E.

Late 8th to 7th		Early 7th to mid 5th		Late 6th to end 4th
Orientalizing		Black-figure		Red-figure
Dipylon Vase 750	Corinithian Amphora Death of a Centaur 700	Warrior Vase (p.10) 650–640	Black-figure amphora Achilles and Ajax 540–530	Death of Sarpedon 510 Red-figure kylix of Dionysus 500

Chapter Two

Sculpture

Although people had been producing carved stone statues and designs for centuries before the ancient Greeks, it was the Greeks who revolutionized the whole approach to sculpture. Within 200 years of starting to make large statues, the Greeks had moved from producing rigid upright sculptures to creating realistic figures shown in a variety of poses. These statues were produced both in stone (usually marble) and bronze, and were used for many purposes. Some of these statues are regarded as being among the finest works of art ever produced.

What Was the Purpose of Sculpture?

Sculpture is found throughout the Greek world and consists of both large and small pieces. Sometimes sculpture was designed for purely decorative purposes, but it was most often used in a religious context. Small carved reliefs (or panels of sculpted stone or terra-cotta) were dedicated in temples as offerings to the gods for their favors. The god of medicine, Asclepius (*Ah-SKLEt-pee-uss*), attracted many such offerings. Often the carvings dedicated to him showed parts of the body that he was believed to have healed. For example, a man whose bad foot had healed would dedicate a carved plaque of a foot. Other offerings to gods might include small

This carving comes from the pediment of the Temple of Zeus at Olympia and was made around 460 B.C.E. A bride is being snatched away from her bridegroom. Her stance shows that she does not want to go with her abductor, who is a centaur (half-man and half-horse).

How Do We Define "Greek" Art?

When art historians or archaeologists discuss Greek art, the earliest form of sculpture from Greece is generally not considered alongside later Greek works from the eighth century B.C.E. onward. Why is this? The earliest carved statues found in Greece come from the Cyclades (*Sigh-CLAD-eez*), a group of islands in the Aegean Sea (between modern Greece and Turkey). These small statues are called "Cycladic figures" and were made between 2800 and 2300 B.C.E. Very little is known about these figures, or whether they represent gods or humans. It is not clear whether or not later Greeks knew anything about them. As a result, many historians believe that later Greek art cannot have been influenced by this sort of sculpture. Thus, historians prefer to limit their discussion about the development of Greek art to periods where it is clear that Greek artists could learn from, and react to, earlier works.

Cycladic figures were made of a shiny white marble, which was ground to the desired shape. Carvings of both men and women exist, but the figures are very stylized.

statuettes of the god or, if the donor was very rich, a large statue.

City-states also made dedications or provided the money to build statues of the gods. One of the largest statues in the ancient world was the great gold and ivory statue of Athena. It was over 40 feet (12 meters) tall and must have dominated the inside of the Parthenon (the temple where it was situated). Various Greek writers describe the statue as dressed in a robe and draped with a goatskin cloak, which had a fringe of snakes around the outside. The figure also had a crested helmet and carried a shield and a spear. This statue of Athena was made between 447 and 438 B.C.E., by one of the finest ancient Greek sculptors, Pheidias (*FI-dee-ass*). Pheidias also made the gold and ivory statue of Zeus at the Temple of Zeus in Olympia, which was one of the Seven Wonders of the Ancient World.

This reconstruction of the great statue of Athena shows how it must have dominated the inside of the Parthenon. Over 2,500 pounds (1,100 kilograms) of gold was used on the statue. Athena holds a small statue of the goddess of victory in her right hand, and a shield in her left.

As well as statues placed inside temples, there was also much sculpture on the outside. This sculpture could be found on three particular areas of temples. First there was the inner frieze (or series of carvings) running around the inner section of a temple, below the roof. Then there were carvings on a series of small sections called metopes (*MEH-toh-pays*), which were also positioned below the roof, but ran around the outer part of the temple. These carvings were not freestanding, but were attached to the temple itself. There was also a triangular shape at the two ends of the temple, called the pediment. Although there was more space for carvings on the pediment, it was not possible to portray a continuous story as could be done on a frieze.

Sculpture on the outside of temples often showed stories from mythology, or specific aspects of the life of the god to whom the temple was dedicated. For example, the Parthenon frieze showed the Panathenaia (*Pa-na-then-EYE-uh*), a great procession held every four years in honor of the goddess Athena. The pediments of the Parthenon portrayed the birth of Athena, as well as the contest between Athena and the sea-god, Poseidon, over who was to become the patron god or goddess of Athens.

How Were Stone Statues Made?

Most statues from ancient Greece were carved out of marble. There is a good supply of marble throughout Greece and, although it is a hard stone to work, it can be polished to a very high

How Did Greek Statues Survive from Antiquity?

The Greeks produced a vast number of statues, but only a tiny fraction of the original number has survived. This loss rate is partly owing to the materials from which they were made. The very earliest statues were carved out of wood, which rotted over time. Later statues were made out of marble or bronze, but marble is easily broken and bronze can be melted down and reused.

Some of the earliest Greek marble statues survived for an unusual reason. When the Persians invaded Greece in 480 B.C.E., they sacked Athens and burned the city. When the Athenians returned to their city, they wanted to rebuild the walls on the Acropolis (or central high point of Athens). Many of the damaged statues were used as rubble in the reconstruction of the walls. These statues survived there for centuries, preserved from vandals and looters, until archaeologists discovered and excavated them.

When the Romans gained control over Greece, they were very much influenced by Greek art. A vast amount of Greek art was shipped to Rome, where it was greatly admired. The Romans produced copies of many of the most famous Greek statues, and these copies enable modern historians to gain some idea of what the originals were like. Moreover, the sea journey between Greece and Italy was difficult and many ships sank on the way. Some fine Greek art has been discovered by marine archaeologists investigating ancient shipwrecks.

degree. Large marble statues took a long time to carve—modern estimates suggest that they may have taken between six months and a year. Naturally, no sculptor wanted to waste an entire year's work, or the expensive marble necessary to create a statue. Therefore, early sculptors worked with a special method, called a grid plan, to avoid making mistakes.

When a grid plan was used, lines were drawn on a rectangular stone block. These lines created a grid on all four sides of the block. The outline of the statue was then drawn on the front, the back, and the two sides. The grid helped to ensure that the statue had the correct proportions on all sides. For example, if the right knee appeared on the fourth square up at the front, it would also appear at the same height on the sides and the back. The sculptor now had a basic pattern to follow to ensure that the various bits of his statue would match up. Carving the statue could now begin by chipping away the stone with a rough tool until the basic shape of the statue was revealed.

The Archaic Smile

On many of the statues from the Archaic period, the lips are turned up, resembling some sort of smile. It seems likely that the first sculptors to carve the smile had no intention of making their statues look happy; it was merely a method of making them look more lifelike.

This figure of a woman was carved around 530 B.C.E. and is brightly painted. Holes in her ear lobes show where earrings would have been attached to the statue.

Egyptian Influence

Not only was the grid plan for carving statues copied from the Egyptians, but also the earliest types of statues were heavily influenced by Egyptian art. This influence occurred because of the increased trade and travel within the Mediterranean region. By the seventh century B.C.E., Greeks were in regular contact with Egypt. Greek mercenary soldiers served in Egypt and trade had increased to such an extent that there was a Greek trading town established at Naucratis (*NAW-krah-tiss*) in Egypt. The Greeks who visited Egypt would have seen the massive granite statues of pharaohs in Egyptian temples. It is not surprising that, soon after the Greeks established links with Egypt, they were producing large sculptures similar to Egyptian statues.

The sculptor would then use increasingly fine chisels to cut away smaller areas of stone. He would also use abrasive powder to rub down the finest details on the marble and to polish the stone to a high shine.

Sometimes sculptors went to the quarry in order to carve the block of marble to the rough shape of the statue. It was easier, and cheaper, to transport a partly carved block to a workshop where the detailed and delicate work of cutting, chiseling, and polishing would be carried out.

Decorative Features

Greek statues from antiquity normally survive in the creamy-white color of their original marble. However, when these statues were first made, they were often painted. Bright colors were used to show details of clothes, hair, and the face. In Greek art, women's flesh was conventionally shown as lighter than men's. White paint may have been used on female sculptures, just as it was used to portray women on vases. Eyes were painted in vibrant colors, or were sometimes made out of glass or ivory and inlaid into the statue. This enabled sculptors to make their statues more realistic, as the eyes could have both an iris and a pupil.

Other details were also added. In their original form, statues often held weapons or wore crowns or jewelry, held in place by small pegs. The pegs would have fit into small holes in the statue. Where such holes survive, it is possible to tell that there had originally been extra features on the statue. For example, there are holes on the carved horses on the Parthenon frieze. These holes would have been used to attach bronze bridles to the horses. The bridles have not survived, but the holes are still there, and their existence enables archaeologists to reconstruct where the bridles would have been placed.

Early Stone Statues—The Archaic Period, 750–480 B.C.E.

Although small statues were made in the eighth century B.C.E., the first large statues to survive from ancient Greece date from the seventh century B.C.E. These figures closely resemble monumental Egyptian statues and were heavily influenced by them. Archaic statues are very stiff and formal. The pose consists of an upright figure, which faces the viewer full-on. One leg

The Story of Kleobis and Biton

The historian Herodotus (*Her-OH-duh-tuss*) records the story of Kleobis and Biton. These two young men lived in Argos, in mainland Greece. Their mother was a priestess at the temple of Hera, the wife of Zeus, the ruler of the gods. One day, the mother was due to go to a festival at the temple, but the oxen that were supposed to pull her cart did not turn up. The temple was 6 miles (10 kilometers) away from the center of Argos and it was impossible for her to find new oxen to drag the cart. However, her two sons were extremely strong and they offered to pull the cart for their mother. When they reached the temple, their mother prayed to Hera to reward her two sons for their devotion and to give them the greatest gift the gods could bestow. Hera listened, although the consequence was perhaps not what the young men's mother intended. After Kleobis and Biton had taken part in the festival, they went to sleep in the temple, and never woke up. Hera had caused them to die in their sleep after carrying out an act of religious devotion.

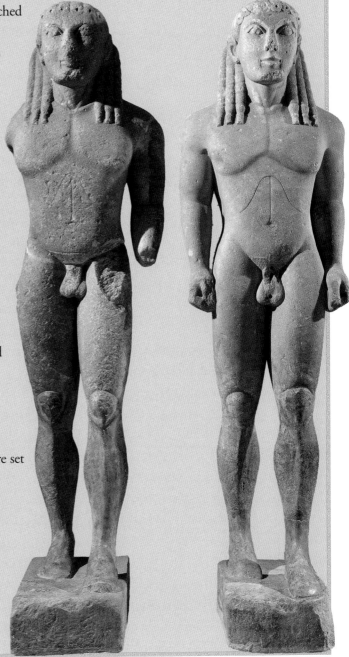

The inhabitants of Argos wished to commemorate the deeds of the two young men and paid a sculptor to create two statues of them. These were dedicated at the sanctuary of Delphi. We might have expected the statues to have been dedicated at the temple of Hera in Argos, but obviously the citizens of Argos were sufficiently proud of Kleobis and Biton to want their fame spread throughout Greece. Therefore the statues were set up at Delphi, which was an international religious site, attracting visitors from across Greece.

Kleobis and Biton. These early Greek statues are 7 feet (2 meters) tall and were made around 580 B.C.E. in the mainland Greek state of Argos.

Kouros and Kore

"Kouros" (KOO-ross) and *"kore" (KOH-ray)* are words in ancient Greek which originally meant a young man and a girl. However, in art they refer to the early type of statue popular in the Archaic period. A male statue is referred to as a *kouros* statue and a female statue is called a *kore* statue. It is estimated that by the time the kouros type of statue lost popularity there were about 20,000 of them erected throughout the Greek world.

is normally slightly extended, but there is little appearance of movement. These statues usually portray young men or young women. Only the men are naked; the women wear heavy clothes, which hang down from their shoulders.

Most of the statues from the Archaic period appear to have been of single figures. However, an unusual set of two *kouros* statues survives. The two young men are called Kleobis (*Klee-OH-bis*) and Biton (*BITT-on*) and were carved around 580 B.C.E. The figures are very robust and give the impression of strength and toughness. This is perhaps deliberate as the two men were said to have been very strong in real life. However, the carving lacks the delicacy of later sculpture and the hair, in particular, looks heavy. There is some movement about the mouth, but the faces remain squat and broad, without much detail.

By the middle of the sixth century B.C.E., Greek sculptors were starting to experiment with different poses. This can be seen in the statue known as the Calf-Bearer. Here, although the legs and body of the statue are in a similar position to kouros statues, the arms are used very differently. The man is carrying a calf on his shoulders, either an animal he has won at an athletic contest or a calf that is to be sacrificed to the gods.

During the sixth century, the features of the kouros statue became increasingly realistic and carving became much more detailed. Faces became smoother and more natural looking and bones no longer jutted out of the face. Eyes were still well-defined, but they began to be more delicately carved. By around 530 B.C.E., human figures were carved in greater detail and showed much more subtle curves of flesh. By the early fifth century B.C.E., although the kouros stance was still being used, statues were significantly more lifelike than earlier statues, such as those of Kleobis and Biton. The statue known as the Critian Boy shows the contrast. There is little to connect the delicate carving of this statue from 490 to 480 B.C.E. with heavier, early work. The hair is much more realistic and the face is sensitively portrayed. The head is turned at a slight angle and the overall impression is of a relaxed and convincingly presented young man.

Changes in Posture and the Classical Period, 480–323 B.C.E.

By the end of the sixth century B.C.E., the carving of flesh and faces had become so realistic that the stiff upright pose of the kouros statue looked odd in comparison. In the early fifth

The Calf-Bearer was dedicated by a man called Rhombus around 560 B.C.E. This is one of the earliest statues dedicated on the Acropolis at Athens.

This statue, known as the Critian Boy, was made around 490 to 480 B.C.E. out of highly–polished marble. The eyes are lost, but would have been made separately (probably out of ivory) and then inserted into the eye sockets.

century B.C.E., the Greeks started to free themselves from the restrictions of the kouros type of statue. Part of the driving force for change came from statues made of bronze. With marble, it is important for limbs to have some sort of support. If not, they have a tendency to break off under their own weight. This makes it difficult to experiment with new poses for free-standing statues—there is no point in creating a revolutionary new shape if the arms are going to break off! However, bronze does not snap under its own weight. Moreover, bronze statues were first modeled in clay, so it was easy for sculptors to experiment with new shapes. These new designs for bronze sculpture were increasingly adventurous and it seems that sculptors working in stone soon wished to create a similar realism in their figures.

Another influence came from experiments in temple sculpture. Some of the carved decoration of a temple was fitted into the triangular section above the temple entrance, called the pediment. Because of the triangular shape, it was impossible to have upright statues all the way along, and Greek sculptors showed considerable ingenuity in designing figures that would fit into the triangular shape. A particularly useful pose was that of a dying or wounded warrior. Because he was dying, he was shown lying down. He therefore fit neatly into the narrow end of the triangle, without appearing to do anything unnatural. It was much easier to carve this sort of statue when it was attached to a temple wall. Instead of having to stand upright and support itself, the statue was supported by the temple itself. Such experiments with shapes helped to encourage sculptors to produce free-standing statues in more challenging and realistic poses.

In the fifth century B.C.E., sculptors broke away from the formal kouros pose. They still produced upright figures, but these were no longer stiff and unwieldy. Instead, the head was carved turned to one side and one hip was slightly raised. These slight adjustments meant that the statue was no longer symmetrical, and it did not stare straight forward. Instead, it appeared to be moving. Another change was in the portrayal of clothes, particularly on women. Women wore long, flowing robes and these presented the sculptor with exciting opportunities. No longer did clothes hang straight down, but the rippling effect of the draperies could be used to suggest living flesh underneath. The desire for realism continued into the fourth century B.C.E. More emotion began to be shown on faces and sculptors tried to make their statues simple and convincing.

The Hellenistic Period, 323–31 B.C.E.

In the Hellenistic Period, after the death of Alexander the Great in 323 B.C.E., there were new forms and new ideas in both literature and art. In sculpture, this experimentation consisted of carving different types of figures. Instead of the idealized youths and maidens of the Archaic Age and the gods and goddesses of the Classical era, Hellenistic sculptors began to produce a variety of statues drawn from real life. In particular, they were ready to carve subjects which

This image of the goddess Artemis comes from the Parthenon frieze and dates to the 440s B.C.E. The sculptor has experimented with the pose of the body in a way in which he could not with a freestanding statue. Such experimenting helped to drive forward the development of more realistic free-standing statues.

The Winged Victory of Samothrace, on display in the Louvre, Paris. Archaeologists are not sure exactly when the statue was made and estimates vary from 300 B.C.E.–190 B.C.E.

The Figure of Victory

The Greeks believed that there was a goddess called Nike (*NEE-keh*), or Victory, who brought victory in battle. In the late fifth century B.C.E., a statue was carved that showed Victory arriving to announce success. This image proved popular and was used many times in later art. One famous example of this design is the Winged Victory of Samothrace (*SAM-oh-thrays*). This statue showed a female figure landing on the front of a ship. The swirling draperies and the feathers of the wings give the impression of a goddess sweeping down through the sky.

were thought to be unattractive, such as barbarians and elderly or wounded people. Indeed, in some sculptors were happy to show broken noses, missing teeth or blood oozing out of cuts in their efforts to make their subjects appear to be as realistic as possible.

Another influence on art of the Hellenistic period was the life of Alexander the Great. In the late fourth century B.C.E., Alexander had conquered the Persian Empire and great swathes of Asia had fallen to Greek control. Alexander had consistently used art as propaganda and he was regularly portrayed on coins and statues in a "heroic" pose, looking noble, brave and wise. Not only did later Greek rulers also wish to be portrayed in this heroic style, but the new Greek kingdoms which sprung up after Alexander's death had a great deal of wealth at their disposal. Their rulers were patrons of the arts and employed sculptors and architects to beautify their cities. Thus Greek art spread throughout much of the old Persian Empire, as well as the original Greek city-states.

This fifth-century B.C.E. bronze statue shows either Zeus, the ruler of the gods, or Poseidon, the god of the sea.

The "Lost Wax" Method

The lost wax method required several stages of work. First, a clay model was made of the statue. Long pins were stuck into the clay and it was left to dry. Then wax was covered over the clay model and carved to the precise shape of the statue. Finally, more clay was plastered over the wax. The long pins helped to keep this clay in place. The clay was then heated and the wax melted. The wax was drained off, leaving a space between the two clay cores. Bronze was then melted and poured into the gap between the clay. When it cooled down, it set in the shape of the melted wax, preserving all the details of the carving. Finally, the clay was removed and the bronze statue remained.

Bronze Statues

As well as marble statues, the Greeks produced large numbers of bronze statues. Bronze is a metal alloy created by adding tin to copper to strengthen it. Bronze working underwent a number of improvements over time. Early bronze statues were made by hammering down thin sheets of bronze on top of a wooden base. The wooden base had already been carved and the bronze merely acted as a kind of top coat. Later, the Greeks developed a method of casting bronze in molds. Molds created solid statues, but were very expensive to use as they required a lot of bronze to make even a small statue. The most effective method for making larger statues is called the "lost wax" method.

Bronze was an excellent material to work with. It was more suitable than marble for making statues because it

The life-size Charioteer of Delphi holds the reins of the horses he once controlled. In the original group, there would have been horses as well as a man, but they have been lost.

This statue was one of a pair of warriors made around the middle of the fifth century B.C.E. The curls of the hair and the beard were cast separately and then attached to the main sculpture.

did not break under its own weight, as marble often did. Moreover, it was possible to build a large statue by casting hollow sections separately and then joining them together. There was, therefore, a much greater freedom of choice in what to create when using bronze. Greek sculptors were not slow to use this freedom.

Statues did not always occur as single figures. The Charioteer of Delphi (*see* page 36) was originally part of a much larger group, which would have included horses, as well as the charioteer who controls them. This work was dedicated at Delphi in the 470s B.C.E. to celebrate a victory at the games held there. The head is turned at an angle and the body is slightly twisted. The charioteer is wearing a long robe and the folds are clearly shown.

By the middle of the fifth century B.C.E., bronze workers were creating statues in all kinds of poses. One of the most striking figures is a bronze god (*see* page 35), made between 470 and 450 B.C.E. It is not known whether the god was supposed to be Zeus or Poseidon, and the weapon he was hurling in his right hand has been lost. If the god represented Zeus, he would have been throwing a thunderbolt, but if he represented Poseidon, the god of the sea, he would have been throwing a trident. This statue is one of the masterpieces of Greek art. The anatomical detail of the body is accurately portrayed and the hair and beard are modeled in

This statue of a horse and his rider was made during the third or second centuries B.C.E. and was recovered from an ancient shipwreck. The face of the boy-jockey shows how bronze could be used to portray human emotions.

This graceful Sphinx from the island of Naxos was made around 560 B.C.E. and was dedicated at Delphi, an important religious site on mainland Greece. Note the careful carving on the wings and chest.

fine detail. The statue conveys a sense of great power and strength. It must surely have been an object of great awe when it was first put on display.

Bronze statues were not painted as marble statues were. However, there was scope for decoration using other metals. For example, the Charioteer of Delphi had a silver headband and the bronze warriors found in a shipwreck near Riace (*Ree-AH-chay*) in Italy had copper lips and silver teeth. Eyes were usually made of glass or ivory, and were set into the bronze face after it had been cast. Sometimes bronze eyelashes were even attached to make the image more realistic.

One of the most impressive bronze statues to survive from ancient Greece is the group known as the Artemision (*Arr-teh-MEEZ-ee-on*) Horse and Jockey (*see* page 38). Archaeologists are not certain exactly where the boy should sit on the horse, but it seems clear that he is a young jockey urging his mount on to victory. This statue was probably dedicated to commemorate a victory in the Olympic Games. The straining muscles of the horse are matched by the determination on the face of the boy, suggesting energy, power, and the will to win.

Other Types of Sculpture

Most of the sculpture shown in this chapter has been of temple decoration or free-standing statues of human beings. However, the Greeks used sculpture in other ways. For example, when the Athenians made their laws, some of them were published so that all could see and read them. Such laws were inscribed on stone and the inscriptions were sometimes topped by small carved figures to represent the democracy of Athens. Sculpture was also very important for commemorating the dead. The memory of famous men might be preserved through statues, but the most common way to remember the dead was through gravestones. Many of these survive, showing the same care and detail in their carving that are found in large statues dedicated in temples. Most of the best examples come from Athens.

The Greeks did not just carve human figures, but also mythological beasts. Sometimes these were used to decorate temples, as on the Temple of Artemis in Corfu. In the center of the pediment of this temple, there was a large carving of Medusa, the gorgon whose glance turned

2800–2300 B.C.E.	700 B.C.E.	600 B.C.E.		500 B.C.E.
Early Bronze Age		Archaic Period		
Cycladic figures 2800–2300		Kleobis and Biton 580 The Calf-Bearer 560 Naxos Sphinx 560	Archaic Woman 530	Critian Boy 490–480 Temple of Zeus Centaur 460 Bronze Warrior 450

men to stone. Another popular beast was the sphinx (a winged creature with a woman's face, but the body of a lion). The image of a sphinx was regularly used on Archaic tombstones, but was also carved elsewhere as a creature in its own right. A fine example of such a beast is the "Sphinx of the Naxians," which takes its name from the fact that it was dedicated by the islanders of Naxos, at the religious site of Delphi. This sphinx, dating from the Archaic period, has the same bland expression found on many statues of humans produced at this time.

Developments in bronze working enabled the Greeks to produce very tall statues. The biggest of these was known as the Colossus of Rhodes, and was over 100 feet (30 meters) tall. It was erected to thank the gods for the fact that the city of Rhodes had survived a siege in 304 B.C.E. This huge statue collapsed in an earthquake some time in the 220s B.C.E.

The Colossus was a huge bronze statue of the sun-god Helios (HE-lee-oss). It had rays coming out of its head representing the sun and stood at the entrance to the harbor at Rhodes.

Over a thousand years after the Colossus collapsed, it took a thousand camels to transport the scrap metal away to be melted down and reused.

It is not known exactly what the Colossus looked like, but it was said to be so large that ships could sail underneath its outstretched legs.

400 B.C.E.	300 B.C.E.	200 B.C.E.	100 B.C.E.
Classical Period	Hellenistic Period		

300?
Winged Victory of Samothrace

292–280
Colossus of Rhodes

Chapter Three

Painting, Jewelry, and Coins

The production of coins and jewelry provided another opportunity for Greek craftsmen to show off their creative talents. Moreover, there was a close link between paintings and mosaics. Mosaics often copied original paintings and sometimes provide us with the only evidence for changes in styles in Greek paintings.

Painting in Houses and Public Buildings

Paintings were used to decorate houses, tombs, and public buildings. Most of the earliest surviving examples of decorative wall painting come from Crete and date from 1550 B.C.E. onward. Here, frescoes were used to bring color and interest to rooms. Sometimes a room might be painted entirely in one color; geometric patterns could also be introduced. Black, white, blue, yellow, red, and green were the most common colors. Animals, such as monkeys, cats, or antelopes, were popular, and brightly painted birds and sea life can also be found. Human beings were regularly painted. Pictures survive of fishermen, children fighting each other, and religious scenes involving priestesses and goddesses. One recurring theme was of young men, or women, turning somersaults over the backs of large bulls.

In classical times, painting was regarded as a very important branch of art. However, while there are descriptions of some of these paintings, the originals do not survive.

This fresco, or wall painting, dates to the late Bronze Age and shows a priestess. This is one of the earliest examples of Greek painting.

We know that a "four-color" technique was introduced, using brown, red, black, and white paint. Artists were said to have been capable of displaying emotion very effectively with only this limited range of colors. During the Classical period, paintings were often used to decorate public buildings. Although these have all been lost, ancient authors provide us with some idea of what they would have looked like. For example, there was a long colonnade (or stoa) in Athens that was famous for its paintings. One of these paintings showed the Athenian victory at the Battle of Marathon in 490 B.C.E. A description of the painting was made by the second century C.E. travel writer, Pausanias (*Pow-SAY-nee-uss*). On the flanks of the battle, the fighters on opposing sides were evenly matched, but in the center, the Persians were losing the fight

Why Do So Few Paintings Survive From the Ancient Greek World?

Ancient painting was created by applying paint to the plaster of buildings. However, very few buildings from antiquity survive complete. If a building collapsed, the painting on its walls would also be lost, or survive only in fragments. Moreover, even where paint was applied directly to stone, thousands of years of exposure to wind and the elements would all but erase any work. The paintings from antiquity that survived best are those found inside tombs. Tombs were dug into the ground and were therefore less inclined to collapse in earthquakes or be destroyed in war. However, tomb paintings could be damaged by damp conditions in the earth.

This painting of a diver dates from around 480 B.C.E. and comes from Paestum (modern Salerno, Italy). Coffins, as well as tombs, could also be painted.

and had started to flee to their ships. In their desperation to reach safety, some Persians thrust their comrades into a marsh as they hurtled past them. Others were shown being captured and slaughtered by vengeful Greeks. Clearly, this was a vivid painting, full of action and excitement and, although it was famous in antiquity, it is one of many such lively pictures that have all been lost.

Tomb Painting

More and more tombs are being discovered by archaeologists in Macedonia, in the far north of ancient Greece. Rich Macedonian Greeks liked to be buried in painted tombs. Sometimes these tombs were decorated to resemble fine buildings, with columns and pediments like those of temples. At other times, scenes from mythology were shown on the walls. Decorated tombs were also popular in Italy, where there were many Greek communities. The Etruscans, who had lived in Italy before the Greek colonists arrived, also had a culture of tomb painting and employed many Greek artists to decorate their burial chambers. Some of the best preserved examples of ancient Greek painting have been found in these graves.

Mosaics

Mosaics are made up of small pieces of colored stone fitted together to make a picture or a pattern. As mosaics were generally set into the floors of buildings, they have survived in much greater numbers than wall paintings, which often disintegrated when a building was destroyed. Mosaics help to show what kinds of images were popular with the ancient Greeks,

This mosaic of a hunting scene was found in Pella, the capital of Macedonia. It was made of pebbles in the late fourth century B.C.E.

and they also reveal some of the techniques of Greek painting. For example, a hunting mosaic from the Macedonian palace of Pella (*see* page 45) shows a scene full of life and vigor. The lion is drawn back, waiting to be attacked by the youth on the right. This young man's cloak billows out behind him, showing that he is moving. The other young man has also drawn his sword and puts his weight on one foot, ready to spring into action. Although mosaics can lack the convincing realism of paintings, this one clearly shows the tension in the muscles of both the men, as well as the lion.

Gold and Jewelry

Despite the fact that few paintings have survived from the ancient Greek world, other forms of Greek art have been found in great numbers. There are many objects made from precious metals. Jewelry was popular in ancient Greece, just as it is today. Greek women liked to adorn themselves with beautiful objects. Men, too, used gold for decoration. In particular, some men wore gold brooches to fasten cloaks. Gold wreaths, fashioned to resemble the leaves of oak or other plants, have been found in the graves of some rich men. Other important finds have also come from tombs, particularly from Mycenaean burials (dating from around the sixteenth to the twelfth century B.C.E.).

This signet ring was made in the fifteenth century B.C.E. and shows offerings being made to a goddess. The picture has been enlarged to show the detail of the engraving—in reality the ring is just over two inches (five centimeters) long.

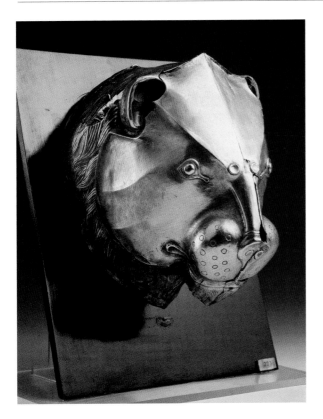

This gold rhyton (*RI-ton*), or drinking cup, was shaped like the head of a lion. Lions were very popular images in Mycenaean art.

The Mycenaeans were skilled metal workers and many examples of excellent gold working have been unearthed from their graves. Important noblemen were buried with rich grave goods. Some had gold death masks covering their faces and carried expensive weapons. Swords often had golden hilts decorated with engraved patterns. Daggers also had gold hilts, but they might additionally have ornate designs running along their edges. This sort of dagger often had geometric patterns, or portrayed sea or hunting scenes.

As well as weapons and death masks, Mycenaean graves have provided examples of costly drinking cups and containers. These vessels were made in a variety of shapes, sizes, and materials. Gold cups could be plain or patterned, and some vessels showed lively scenes of human and animal life. Men are pictured catching bulls, or taking part in agricultural festivals. Wild goats and sea creatures, such as octopuses, also appear. However, not all containers were made in a normal round shape. Some artists liked to display their skill by creating objects in the form of animals or birds. Examples have been found of a crystal bowl in the shape of a duck, a stone vessel carved as a seashell, and a stone drinking vessel made to resemble a bull's head.

Gold jewelry survives from all periods of the Greek era. Women wore a wide range of jewelry. Rings, bracelets, necklaces, brooches, earrings, and hair ornaments, called *diadems*, were popular. Here, too, geometric patterns and the natural world inspired many designs. Flowers and plants were popular and gold representations of ears of wheat have been discovered. Images of gods and goddesses are fairly rare on jewelry, partly because it is hard to portray the human figure on small pieces of metal, and the gods looked very human. Before the death of Alexander the Great in 323 B.C.E., most jewelry was made entirely from metal (normally gold, silver, or a mixture of the two, called *electrum*). However, in the Hellenistic period, after 323 B.C.E., the practice of inlaying semi-precious stones into gold jewelry became increasingly popular.

These two bracelets in the shape of snakes, decorated with semi-precious stones, date from the Hellenistic period. The image of a snake was a popular design on rings and bracelets.

Seal Stones and Coinage

Greek jewelry was often intricate and required considerable skill to make. However, some of the earliest forms of Greek ornament demanded the greatest detail in carving. These forms were seal stones and signet rings. Seal stones were very small stones with a personalized engraving, which served as a mark of someone's identity. A signet ring was used for the same purpose, although it was made from metal rather than stone. These stones and rings first appeared in the sixteenth century B.C.E. and had extremely detailed engraving on a small surface area. What these engravings depict is not always known, but many of them seem to show some sort of religious scene. For example, the illustration on page 46 appears to portray four mythical creatures (which look rather like winged lions) bringing jugs to a female figure, who sits holding a large cup. It is thought that the sitting figure must be a goddess, rather than a priestess, because she is wearing a headdress and a hawk is shown near her. Whatever the role of the female figure, she may well have some connection with agriculture, as ears of corn are shown between the various animals and at the top of the ring.

Seal stones and signet rings belonged to Mycenaean times. As these stones were carved individually and created for one specific person, it is not clear how many people would have been familiar with their designs. However, the importance of detailed engraving on small

1500–1200 B.C.E.	500 B.C.E.			400 B.C.E.
Mycenaean Period	Classical Period			
Signet ring 1400 Gold drinking cup 1300	Athens starts producing coins 570–550	Diver painting 480	Athenian coin c. 450	Hunting mosaic late 4th century

objects became clear when coinage was introduced into Greece in the seventh and sixth centuries B.C.E. Naturally, it was important for each Greek city-state to have its own coinage and there were many different designs among early Greek coins.

The finest ancient Greek coinage came from the colony of Syracuse, on Sicily. However, the most common coins are those from Athens, which had a rich source of silver and was able to produce coins with ease. In the fifth century B.C.E., Athens imposed the same currency throughout her empire. Since all the Greek states knew that Athenian coinage had a standard weight, it was a popular method of payment even in non-Athenian regions. Athenian coins are easily recognizable because they are stamped with the head of Athena on one side and an owl on the other. As well as being the goddess of wisdom, Athena was the patron goddess of Athens and the owl was associated with Athena because it was believed to be a very wise bird. These Athenian "owls" soon spread throughout the Greek world.

Coins from Athens were stamped with Athena's owl. Coins in the ancient Greek world were normally made from silver, although gold coins were issued by Alexander the Great and his successors.

How Were Coins Made?

Unlike signet rings or seal stones, coins could be produced in large numbers with little effort. Until the fourth century B.C.E., nearly all Greek coins were made of silver. This silver was placed between two dies (or carved patterns) and struck by hand. Although each coin was made individually, thousands could be made to exactly the same pattern. Many Greek city-states included their name as part of the design, but some used a symbol that became so well-known that everyone knew by looking at it where the coin had come from. For example, coins with a turtle as their symbol came from the island of Aegina (*Ee-JIE-nuh*).

300 B.C.E.	187 B.C.E.
Hellenistic Period	

Gold spiral bracelet
c. 250

Chapter Four

Houses and Public Buildings

When we talk about Greek architecture, we often think of temples, such as the Parthenon at Athens. However, the Greeks did not just build temples, they had a wide range of buildings, for both domestic and public use.

Houses and Domestic Architecture

Archaeologists try to reconstruct what Greek houses looked like by studying their foundations, but it is not always easy to produce accurate reconstructions of houses, or to know what size most houses would have been. Greek houses were made of sun-dried bricks, rather than stone, and this means that few traces of them have survived to the present day. In particular, it can be difficult to find evidence of houses built in the countryside, because the land on which they were built may have been cleared and used for agriculture. Remains of mosaics are useful to help estimate the size of rooms, but houses with mosaics would have belonged to fairly wealthy people. The size of a house would probably vary according to the wealth of its owner, and it is likely that the houses of the rich would have had many more rooms than the houses of the poor.

Houses seem to have been built of brick on stone foundations. Sometimes the outside of the house was plastered with lime, which was colored white. The roofs were covered with clay tiles, or thatch, and windows would have had wooden shutters, rather than glass. Some houses had a second story with a wooden staircase leading upstairs to the bedrooms and the women's quarters. The kitchen was downstairs, as was the men's dining area. Unless they were attending to chores downstairs, women

The thirteenth-century B.C.E. Lion Gate is part of the city walls at Mycenae. These walls were so large that giants were said to have built them. The entrance to the city is underneath a huge stone carved with the image of two lions.

were expected to stay upstairs, where they could not be seen by men who did not belong to the family. This division of living space was probably more regularly observed in towns than in isolated rural farms, where women might well work in the fields during the day.

Houses in the country were normally attached to farms. There would have been small outbuildings to keep animals, although the very poorest Greeks may have brought their animals to shelter inside their houses at night. In towns, houses had a number of rooms set around a central courtyard. There were few windows facing out onto the street and the entrance to the house was through a porch that led into the central courtyard. In the late fourth century B.C.E., houses became more elaborate. From that time onward, rich people could enjoy gardens, mosaics, and fine wall paintings in their houses.

Public Architecture

Although little domestic architecture survives from ancient Greece, a wide variety of public buildings still exists. The earliest constructions are city walls, which were essential to defend any city from enemy attack. The first large city walls date from Mycenaean times and were

This reconstruction of a Greek house shows a busy town scene. A man is entering the main door of the house and comes into the courtyard. Women are busy weaving clothes or preparing food.

made from enormous stone blocks piled on top of each other. Later Greeks were so awed by the sheer scale of these fortifications that they believed that only giants could have built them. Some of the blocks are 15 feet (4.5 meters) long by 6 feet (2 meters) wide.

As cities began to develop, so did civic architecture. More and more public buildings were built, for political as well as religious purposes. A simple, but very useful, building was the *stoa* (*STO-uh*), which seems to have come into use in the seventh century B.C.E. A stoa was a long rectangular building with a back wall and two side walls. The front was open, with a series of columns running along its length. The roof was supported by these columns and a second row of columns inside the stoa. These colonnaded buildings provided shade from the sun and protection from storms, while still being open to the fresh air. Stoas were a good place to meet people and to gossip, but they could also be used for shops, to house law courts, to commemorate glorious moments in history, or as a shrine to the gods. An entire group of philosophers, the Stoics, took their name from the stoa in which they met to discuss ideas.

Stoas were often found in the *agora* (*ah-GOR-ah*), or marketplace. The agora was a very important part of any Greek town. It consisted of an open space, surrounded by many shops and public

What Does a Doorway Tell Us?

Archaeologists look at the floor plans of houses to decide what the rooms were used for. For example, if there is a hearth in the room, it was probably used for cooking. One key method of recognizing a dining room is the presence of a doorway that is not placed in the center of a wall. The ancient Greeks liked to recline on couches during dinner parties. These couches were placed around the walls of a dining room and the doorway was situated where one couch was missing. The door was therefore not in the center of a wall, but to one side.

Taking Your Doors With You

In most regions of Greece, wood was an expensive commodity. The soil of Greece is not capable of supporting large numbers of trees and there is little wood to build from. Therefore, ancient Greeks tried to build as much as possible from other materials. Stone was ideal for large public buildings, but mud bricks were often used to build houses. However, some parts of the house had to be made of wood, such as the doors or window shutters. This wood was so valuable that when a house was destroyed, the wood was often salvaged and reused. When the Spartans invaded Athens during the Peloponnesian War (431–404 B.C.E.), the Athenians who lived in the countryside moved into the city for safety. They took with them all their belongings, but they also took doors and other wooden parts of their houses because they were so expensive to replace.

This picture shows a representation of the Painted Stoa in Athens. This stoa was famous in antiquity for its wonderful paintings representing incidents in Athenian mythology and history, including the Athenian victory over the Persians at the Battle of Marathon in 490 B.C.E.

buildings. The Athenian agora also contained a temple and the *bouleterion* (*BOO-luh-tay-ree-on*), or council chamber. Athenian councilors met here to decide what business would be put forward for discussion by the entire Athenian assembly of citizens. Agoras were very busy places, because people would visit them not only to shop, but also to exchange news and meet friends.

Theaters and Athletics

A very important part of Greek culture was drama. Plays were regularly performed to large audiences in outdoor theaters across Greece. It was essential for audiences to be able to hear what was being said, and the Greeks designed theaters precisely with this in mind. Theaters were semi-circular in shape and carved out of hillsides. Not only did this give support to the building, but it enabled the spectators to have an excellent view. Moreover, the shape of the theater provided very good acoustics. The sound of the actors' voices was caught in the bowl shape, and was projected back to the farthest row.

Open-air Politics

Most modern democracies build splendid buildings to house their governments, because they want to demonstrate how highly they regard their senates or parliaments. However, Athens, the best-known ancient Greek democracy, did not provide any such building. This was partly due to one major limitation of Greek architecture. Democratic politics require a clear view of what is going on, but the Greeks could only build rooms as wide as the longest roof beam. Anything larger would require the use of many columns, which would make it harder to see and hear speakers. It was, therefore, impossible to create a roofed building large enough to contain the thousands of people who took part in Athenian democratic politics. The Greeks were able to get around this problem by holding meetings in the open air, but in a colder climate this solution would have been impossible. Only when the Romans revolutionized the use of the arch was it possible to create large buildings suitable for mass meetings.

Early theaters did not have stone seating. Audiences either sat on the hillside or on wooden seats. As drama became increasingly popular, stone seats were built in theaters. These seats rose in tiers up the hillside and it is likely that audiences brought cushions to sit on during the performance. Special seats at the front of the theater were reserved for important officials and visitors. In the fourth century B.C.E., a colonnade was introduced behind the circular dancing floor. This colonnade was sometimes used to support a raised stage.

Theaters varied in size. The principal theaters of a city-state would be very large (the theater at Epidauros could hold about 14,000 people), but those that served only local festivals, which fewer people attended, were much smaller. The main theater at Athens was the theater of Dionysus, which was built into the slopes of the Acropolis. It dates from the fifth century B.C.E. and could seat over 20,000 people.

Not all events were held in the theater. In Athens there was an indoor concert hall called the Odeon, which was used for poetry recitations and music competitions. Similar halls were

The theater at Epidauros in mainland Greece is one of the best preserved ancient theaters. It was built around 350 B.C.E. into a natural hill and has excellent acoustics. Originally there were stage buildings at the back of the circular stage.

Poor Olympic Facilities

Nowadays, competitors at the Olympic Games are well-housed in athletes' villages. However, in the ancient Greek world, the site of the Olympic Games at Olympia was well-known for having poor facilities. Accommodations were cramped and there was an inadequate supply of water for bathing. A guest house for important visitors was built at Olympia in the fourth century B.C.E., and a training gymnasium for athletes was added in the third century B.C.E. However, a permanent water supply was only created in the second century C.E. Rather than having to depend on temporary wells, a splendid fountain was built to provide constantly running water.

Many visitors, as well as competitors, came to Olympia. They would crowd through doorways such as this one to reach the race track and palaestra.

The Athenian agora was the center of commerce and business activity, whereas the acropolis was the center of religious activity.

The acropolis, with its many temples, could be seen from the agora.

There were a number of stoas, or colonnaded areas, in the agora. These often contained shops.

found in other cities. Many Greek cities had a sports ground, known as a *gymnasium*, situated outside the city walls. The gymnasium usually consisted of a running track and a *palaestra* (*pal-AI-stra*). The palaestra was a low building with a central courtyard, which was covered with sand. Here boys would receive lessons in wrestling. Some sports grounds also had jumping pits and areas to practice javelin and discus throwing, as well as changing rooms and rooms for ball games.

These types of facilities were found on a larger scale in the religious sanctuaries where the major athletic competitions, such as the Olympic Games, were held. Running events were held in a stadium. This was a long oval shape and had banked rows of seats, as in a theater. Here, too, the first examples of a stadium appear to have been made out of earth and only later were wooden or stone seats added. Other athletic events, such as wrestling and boxing, took place in a small sandy area, often surrounded by a colonnade.

The bouleterion was the council chamber where 500 councilors decided what public business needed to be discussed. The round building next to it was called the Tholos where fifty councilors were always present.

The Temple of Hephaestus was situated in a raised position above the agora. The Greeks believed that Hephaestus was the god of blacksmiths and was a fine craftsman in his own right.

Many craftsmen lived near the agora. In particular, many bronze workers lived near the Temple of Hephaestus.

Chapter Five

Death and Religion

Death and religion were both important aspects of Greek life. Some of the earliest examples of Greek architecture are tombs to hold the dead, and some of the finest Greek buildings are the temples they built for worshipping their gods.

Death and Burial

Some of the strictest rules in human cultures concern the correct treatment of the dead. Different societies have different ways of dealing with the dead, but in nearly all cultures it is vital to carry out the appropriate ritual. Many societies cremate the dead. Others bury their dead in the ground, either in graves dug out of the ground or in specially built tombs. The ancient Greeks carried out both practices. Archaeologists have discovered large tombs, which held the dead person buried whole, as well as the cremated bones of the dead buried in funerary urns (or pots to hold the ashes).

Some of the earliest and best preserved examples of Greek tombs come from ancient Mycenae, in the Peloponnese. Here there were two different types of burial in operation. The first type of burial was in shaft graves, which date from 1600 B.C.E. Shaft graves consisted of a trench dug into the earth and lined with stone at the bottom. The body was placed in the chamber at the bottom of the shaft. Grave goods, such as fine gold jewelery or pots containing oil and perfume, would be

This magnificent tomb, known as the Treasury of Atreus (after a mythical king of Mycenae) was built in the second half of the fourteenth century B.C.E. The block over the entrance is over 26 feet (8 meters) long and weighs over 100 tons.

added for use in the afterlife and then earth would be heaped onto the body. Shaft graves could be up to 13 feet (4 meters) deep and might contain more than one body, probably from the same family. Shaft graves were often located together. One circular burial ground of graves, known as Grave Circle A, was found inside the city walls of Mycenae, and it is thought that these graves probably contained the bodies of the Mycenaean royal family.

Around 1500 B.C.E., the Mycenaeans changed the way they buried their nobles. Instead of digging shaft graves, they began to build large *tholos* (*THAW-loss*) tombs. Tholos tombs are marvels of ancient engineering. A long pathway made of stone called a *dromos* (*DROM-oss*) led up to the entrance of the tomb. The tomb itself was also built of stone, but was not rectangular. Instead, it was shaped like a beehive, with a domed roof that sloped inward. The height of the roof varied, but some examples are over 40 feet (13 meters) high. There was a side chamber, reached from the main tomb. After the body and the grave goods were left in the tomb, the entrance would be closed and the entire tomb covered over with a mound of earth.

The stone used in tholos tombs was carefully prepared. It was cut and dressed (shaped) so that sections joined smoothly and the entrance to the tomb was lavishly decorated. Columns might be used and fragments survive of spirals and flowers carved on stone. There is also evidence that different colored stone, such as green or red, was used to provide contrasts to the usual gray or cream. Some

How Were the Domed Roofs of Tholos Tombs Made?

Tholos tombs are large structures, with some being as much as 50 feet (15 meters) wide. It was essential to provide a roof to cover the tomb and to protect the body, but it would be impossible to build a stone roof over a rectangular space of this width (the largest stones would not span the gap). Therefore, the Mycenaean engineers came up with an ingenious solution. Instead of trying to span the width of the tomb with stone, they reduced the width by a technique known as a corbeled roof. A corbeled roof is one where each layer of the stone wall overlaps the stones in the layer beneath it. As the tomb increases in height, it also shrinks in width. Naturally, this sort of building was made much easier by the rounded shape of the tomb, but it also required considerable care to ensure that the entire structure was stable. In particular, it was vital to make sure that the foundations of the tomb were wide enough to bear the weight of the stone.

This reconstruction of a tholos tomb shows how much weight the roof of the tomb would have had to bear.

Burial for Nobles

Tholos tombs were intended to hold the bodies of the rich and powerful. They must have taken months or years to build and it is likely that they were constructed before the people who were to be buried in them had died. Tholos tombs were a sign of a person's status and importance, not only after death, but also during his or her lifetime, while the tomb was slowly being built. The bodies of the poor would not have received such magnificent tombs. They were probably buried in the earth with just a few pots containing food, rather than the lavish offerings of gold found in the graves of the rich.

The inside of the Treasury of Atreus shows how corbeled roofs were constructed from overlapping courses of stones. Tholos tombs can be found throughout southern Greece, but some of the most impressive are at Mycenae.

tombs may also have been decorated with bronze plaques pinned to the inside.

Later Burials

Later Greeks also wished to bury their dead with formal ceremony, but they did not go to the lengths of the Mycenaeans in constructing such large and magnificent tombs. Instead, they preferred to show the importance of the occupant with large grave markers.

Sometimes these markers consisted of large pottery vases or stone statues erected over the grave. Later, in the Classical period, ancient Greeks placed large tombstones over graves. These were often inscribed with the name of the dead person and a carving illustrating some part of his or her life, such as a woman nursing a baby, or a soldier

This section of the cemetery area of Athens is known as the Street of the Tombs. Impressive sculpted tombstones served to demonstrate the wealth and importance of Athenian families.

The Mausoleum

One of the most famous tombs from antiquity has given its name to a type of tomb. This is the mausoleum, named after the man who ordered that it be made to house his body. Mausolus was the satrap (or governor) of a region of the Persian Empire called Caria (*KAY-ree-uh*). Although Mausolus ruled Caria on behalf of the Persians, he was heavily influenced by Greek ideas and, in any case, had considerable independence of action from the Persians.

Mausolus was very powerful and wanted to celebrate his power even in death. Therefore, he decided to build a magnificent tomb to remind all who saw it of his importance. The mausoleum was designed by Greek architects, and much of it had been built by the time Mausolus died in 353 B.C.E.

Thirty-six columns were built on a high platform. Above the columns was a pyramid, topped by a sculpture of four horses pulling a chariot. There was a frieze around the mausoleum that showed a battle between the Greeks and the legendary warrior-women, the Amazons. Two colossal statues associated with the mausoleum are assumed to be of Mausolus and Artemisia, his widow, who continued to rule Caria after his death. The mausoleum was about 134 feet (41 meters) high, and was one of the wonders of the ancient world. Later Greeks and Romans were greatly impressed by this huge tomb (which only collapsed in an earthquake in the fifteenth century C.E.) and many of their buildings were influenced by the mausoleum and its design.

This Doric temple of Apollo from Corinth was built around 540 B.C.E. The squat columns with plain capitals are clearly visible.

charging on horseback against an enemy. The best evidence for later burials comes from ancient Athens, where an entire area called the Kerameikos (*Ker-ah-MAY-ee-koss*) has been excavated. Part of this area contained a public graveyard, and many fine tombstones have been found there.

Temples

Temples were the finest buildings the Greeks produced. Their basic purpose was to provide a home for the god (or gods) to whom they were dedicated. Temples also came to have other roles, such as a treasury for the Athenians, or as a meeting place for the city councilors at Ephesus. While the main focus of a temple was worship, such splendid buildings were an obvious symbol of a state's power and wealth. Therefore, many ancient Greek city-states poured a great deal of their money into constructing the finest temples they could afford. Athens, in particular, pursued an impressive and imaginative building program in the mid-fifth century B.C.E. This was partly to replace temples damaged or destroyed by the Persians in 480 B.C.E., but it was also a means of demonstrating her power and importance to Greek city-states both in and out of her empire.

How Were Temples Made?

The first Greek temples were small and probably made out of wood. However, from around the seventh century B.C.E., stone became much more commonly used. Marble was the best stone for building temples because it was very strong and provided an excellent surface for carving sculpture. Limestone was also used, although it did not weather as well as marble. In Sicily and Italy, Greek temples might also be built using the local sandstone. The roof was constructed from a timber frame with roof tiles of terra-cotta or stone. Stone coffers, or tiles, could also be carved with geometric patterns and attached to the underside of temple ceilings.

As temples were so large, an enormous amount of energy and money was needed to transport all the necessary materials to the building site. Large blocks of stone were brought from quarries on wagons drawn by oxen. These blocks were dressed by stonemasons using a variety of chisels, hammers, and mallets. When the stones had been sized to the correct shape they were lifted using a system of ropes and pulleys. To make it easier to lift the stone, lumps, known as "lifting bosses," were left sticking out of the block. Ropes could then grip the stone more effectively. These lifting bosses were smoothed away after the block was in its correct position.

To make the temple construction stronger, blocks of stone were held in the correct position by the use of clamps. Clamps were made of metal (usually iron) and linked one block to another. Any inaccuracies in the stonecutting were smoothed off and the stones were given a final polish.

This Ionic column is from the Erechtheum at Athens. The top of the capital, known as the volute, is curved like a ram's horns.

Columns were an important part of the temple. Columns were not carved out of one piece of stone, but from many cylindrical sections, known as column drums. These sections had holes in their centers. When the sections were placed on top of each other, these formed a central shaft into which metal pegs were placed to hold the column drums together. Column drums had carved grooves, called fluting, running down the length of the column. Stonemasons carved the outline of the fluting while the column drums lay on the ground, and it was finished off when the column was in place in the temple. Column drums normally became narrower as they reached the top of the building, so it was important to be able to check that all the sections matched up before the final carving was done. The column was headed with a capital, or carved stone top. These tops varied in complexity and were designed to give a finished appearance to the column.

Entrances to temples were designed to be as grand and awe inspiring as possible. Many temples had a flight of steps leading up to the main entrance, but in the Peloponnese (in southern Greece) temples often had a ramp in place of steps. Temples might also be found in a group, rather than as individual buildings. When this occurred, architects often tried to ensure that the entrance to the temple complex had the maximum visual effect. For example, the Acropolis at Athens is a high rock, which had a series of temples on it. The Greek architects made full use of the height of the Acropolis by designing a monumental stairway leading up to the principal entrance, flanked by sacred buildings. This entrance, built from 437 to 432 B.C.E., was known as the Propylaea (*pro-pi-LAI-ah*). The Propylaea ensured that the visitor was directed through this dramatic entrance before coming out onto the Acropolis itself and seeing all the other buildings.

Styles

Greek temples could be built in different styles with three principal orders. The Doric (*DAW-rik*) order was the earliest and plainest of these. Columns were thicker than in the other orders and the capital, at the top of the column, was plain. In early Doric buildings there is usually no column base.

The Ionic (*Eye-ON-ik*) order originated in the Greek cities of Ionia (the western coastal strip of modern Turkey). It differed from the Doric order, having thinner columns and a decorated capital and base. The capital had a curved head, rather like ram's horns. These swirls are known as *volutes* (*VOL-utes*).

The most elaborate decoration was found on the capital of the Corinthian column. Instead of a plain or curved top, this type of column had carved acanthus leaves all around the capital. Sometimes there were smaller leaves on the bottom, with larger leaves reaching up to the top. According to tradition, a man called Callimachus (*Kal-IM-uh-kuss*) first thought of the design. He looked at a basket hanging over the grave of a young Corinthian woman. The basket was surrounded by acanthus leaves, which were protected by a tile at the top. Callimachus so admired this

How Do Archaeologists Know How Temples Were Made?

Archaeologists use lots of clues to work out how and when buildings were made. For example, they know that lifting bosses were used, because sometimes the bosses have not been smoothed away on areas of stone that would have been hidden from public view (such as the foundations). Therefore, they can argue that lifting bosses were probably used to raise similarly shaped blocks throughout the temple. In the same way, tiny clues can help archaeologists date temples, even if there is little of the temple left. The shape and type of clamp used to link blocks of stone together changed over time. Therefore, archaeologists can assume that if a certain type of clamp is used, the temple is unlikely to date from a period when those clamps were not in use.

The first Corinthian column was used in Greece around 430 B.C.E., but the Corinthian order was particularly popular in Roman times. This example comes from the Temple of Olympian Zeus in Athens and was constructed in the second century C.E.

that he decided to imitate the effect with column capitals. Most Greek temples are Doric or Ionic, but the Corinthian order proved to be very popular with the Romans.

One of the most unusual buildings to survive from ancient Greece is the Erechtheum (*Eh-RECK-thee-um*). This was built on the Acropolis at Athens and is also known as the Temple of Athena Polias (*POLL-ee-ass*), because it once contained a fine statue of Athena in her role as protector of the city. While some of the building follows the plan of a straightforward Ionic temple, the south side is most unusual. Here there is a projecting porch, and the roof of this porch is not supported by normal fluted columns. Instead, the architect decided to use six *caryatids* (*CARRY-ah-tids*), or draped female

Heroes, Tridents, and Sacred Snakes!

The Erechtheum was built on the site of a collection of older sacred buildings, and this makes it difficult for archaeologists to be certain as to the purpose of each section. The name of the temple was derived from Erechtheus, a mythical king of Athens. Erechtheus had been brought up by Athena. When Athens was attacked by Eumolpus (*YOU-moll-pus*), one of the sea-god Poseidon's sons, Erechtheus asked the oracle at Delphi how he could save the city. The oracle replied that if he sacrificed one of his daughters, he would defeat Eumolpus. Erechtheus killed the girl and Athens was saved. However, Poseidon was so angry with Erechtheus that he killed him and the remainder of his family.

Erechtheus was not the only person who was honored at the Erechtheum. Athena and Poseidon were also worshipped here. Indeed, there was part of the ground that had a strange mark in it. This was said to be where Poseidon had struck his trident into the earth to make a well full of seawater, when he and Athena had a contest to see who would be the patron god of Athens. Athena provided the olive tree, the source of much Athenian wealth, and won the competition.

Ancient writers record that there was an altar to Zeus in front of the Erechtheum. Here nobody was allowed to sacrifice anything that breathed, or pour wine during ceremonies. Instead, sweet honey cakes would be left on the altar. Sacred snakes would crawl out of the nearby snake pit and eat the honey cakes. In the time of the Persian Wars, one of the Athenian leaders, Themistocles, wanted Athens to be evacuated because he knew that the Athenians were not strong enough to resist the Persians. One day, the offerings put out for the sacred snake were not eaten and Themistocles stated that if the sacred snake had left the Erechtheum Athena wanted the evacuation to take place. Athens was then evacuated.

These caryatids (or female figures) serve to hold up part of the roof of the Erechtheum. The temple was built between 421 and 405 B.C.E.

figures. The caryatids were carved out of stone with a capital on top of their heads. The capitals provided a flat surface to bear the weight of the roof of the building. Caryatids were rarely used in Greek architecture, but they were a very decorative means of providing structural support.

The Parthenon

The Parthenon, built to honor Athena, is one of the finest temples to survive from the ancient Greek world. The Parthenon stands on the site of an earlier temple, destroyed by the Persians when they invaded Greece in 480 B.C.E. At first the Athenians swore an oath not to replace the burned buildings on the Acropolis until the Persians had been punished. However, as Athens' empire expanded and her political power grew, many Athenians felt that the time had come to replace the buildings destroyed by the Persians.

The Temple of the Maiden

The Parthenon was built in honor of Athena and its name also honors Athena. "Parthenos" is the ancient Greek word for an unmarried maiden and to call Athena's temple the Parthenon was a method of showing that she was worshipped here in her role as an unmarried woman.

Other temples bore names that referred to other attributes of Athena. For example, there were two other temples dedicated to Athena on the Acropolis. These were the Temple of Athena Nike (or Athena of Victory) and the Temple of Athena Polias (or City Athena), which housed an ancient sacred olivewood statue of Athena. Temple names might also refer to geography. The temples of Athena at Sounium (*SOO-nee-um*) and Pallene (*Pah-LEE-nee*) were called the temples of Athena Sounias and Athena Pallenis to show that Athena was being worshipped in these places.

One of the driving forces behind the ambitious Athenian building program was Pericles. He was repeatedly elected to run Athens during the mid-fifth century B.C.E. Pericles believed that the finest architects and craftsmen should work to create public buildings that reflected the importance of Athens. Much of the money to pay for this building program came from members of the Athenian Empire. Some people in Athens did not agree with this. However, many Athenians believed that since Athens provided the ships to protect the empire from attack, it was reasonable for imperial money to be spent replacing temples in the imperial capital. Part of this money was spent in building the Parthenon over a fifteen-year period from 447 to 432 B.C.E.

What made the Parthenon an exceptional temple was a combination of size and quality. At the time it was built, the Parthenon was the largest temple on the Greek mainland, measuring 228 feet (70 meters) by 237 feet (72 meters). Only the temple of Olympian Zeus at Athens, finished some six centuries later, was larger, measuring some 352 feet (107 meters) by 135 feet (41 meters). The Parthenon was also built by expert craftsmen, who took considerable care in its construction. The white marble stones from which it was made were dressed so carefully that

Temples varied in size, but followed a basic plan of columns on a raised platform, with an inner central section that contained the cult-statue of a god. This reconstruction shows a temple from Selinus, a Greek city on the south coast of Sicily.

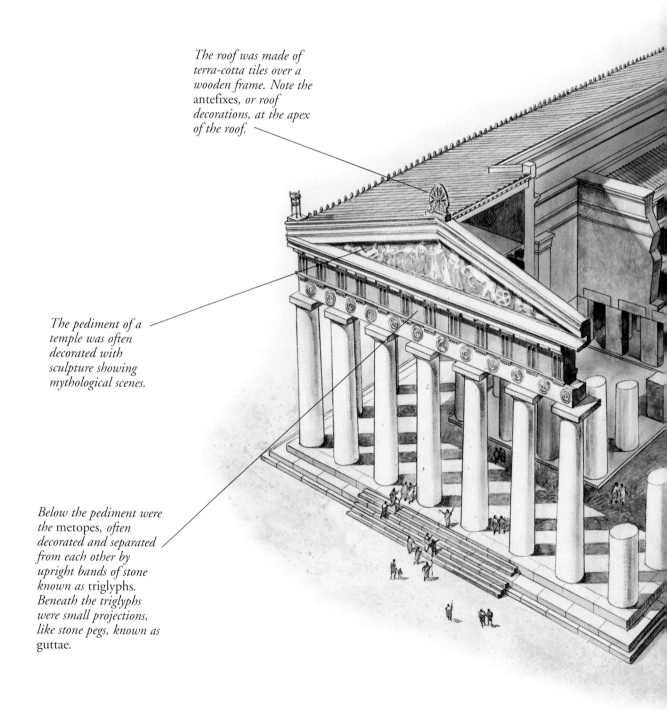

The roof was made of terra-cotta tiles over a wooden frame. Note the antefixes, *or roof decorations, at the apex of the roof.*

The pediment of a temple was often decorated with sculpture showing mythological scenes.

Below the pediment were the metopes, *often decorated and separated from each other by upright bands of stone known as* triglyphs. *Beneath the triglyphs were small projections, like stone pegs, known as* guttae.

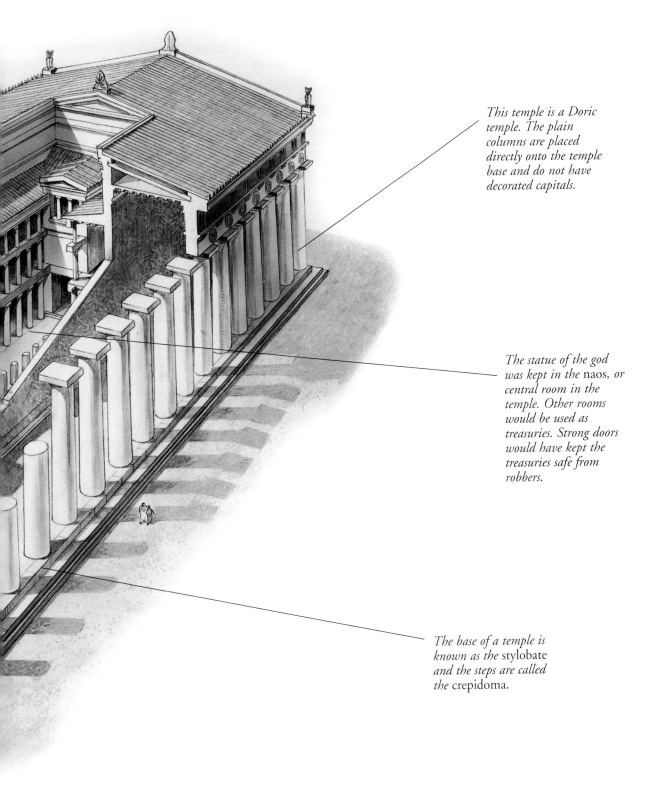

This temple is a Doric temple. The plain columns are placed directly onto the temple base and do not have decorated capitals.

The statue of the god was kept in the naos, or central room in the temple. Other rooms would be used as treasuries. Strong doors would have kept the treasuries safe from robbers.

The base of a temple is known as the stylobate and the steps are called the crepidoma.

the joints between the blocks hardly showed. The architect Ictinus (*IK-tee-nuss*) used mathematics to ensure that his design looked perfect. The Parthenon is deceptive in its appearance. Its columns look straight, but are actually slightly tapered. Similarly, the horizontal elements of the temple appear to be at the same height, but in reality they curve gently upward. Such careful planning results in a structure of considerable visual impact.

The Parthenon is a Doric temple. Although this means that its columns are topped with undecorated capitals, other parts of the temple

Treasuries at Sacred Sites

Not only did the Greeks have treasuries in their own city-states, but treasuries were also built at important centers of religion, such as Delphi. These treasuries were often designed like miniature temples, and were used to house gifts given to the gods. It was a matter of pride to build a fine treasury, which showed the wealth of a city-state. Individuals might also set up votive monuments to give thanks to the gods, often when they had won an important race or athletic contest.

were highly decorated. The two pediments (triangular spaces at each end of the temple) had sculptures representing the birth of Athena and the contest between Athena and Poseidon.

Most Greek temples survive now in the color of their natural stone. However, when they were first built they would have been brightly painted. These restorations show what some parts of the Parthenon might have originally looked like.

The procession of cavalry is finely carved, but the detail would also have been painted. The bridles of the horsemen would have been made of bronze and added to the sculpture after it had been carved.

The three patterns above the horsemen would also have been painted. These patterns would have wound their way around the entire frieze.

The Parthenon was blown up in 1687 C.E. Much of the decoration was badly damaged. These three statues of goddesses survive without their heads.

This detail of a goddess' robe shows how the painting reflected the folds of the carving.

Originally, the statues were painted. Clothes and hair would have been shown in bright colors. Details of the cheeks and other parts of the flesh would have used more delicate shades.

The background would also have been painted to make a good backdrop to the statues.

The Parthenon dominates the Acropolis at Athens. It is built on a man-made platform and can be seen from many miles away.

Underneath the pediments a frieze ran around the outside of the building. There was also a second series of carvings on the metopes directly above the columns. The frieze was an uninterrupted carving, but the metopes came in small sections, each of which was separated from the next by three carved upright bands called *triglyphs* (*TRIG-liffs*). These carvings showed a procession in honor of Athena and scenes of battle from mythology. All of the carving was positioned at a considerable height from the viewer on the ground. However, it would have been painted different colors and would have stood out well in the intense Greek sunlight.

Politics in Art?

The Parthenon was one of many buildings built to replace originals destroyed during the Persian invasion of Greece. The replacement buildings sometimes had decorative elements reflecting the recent violent past. For example, the carvings on the metopes of the Parthenon show a mythological battle between Lapiths (*LAP-iths*), a legendary race of men, and centaurs (men with the bodies of horses). Many people believe that this story was chosen because it could represent the struggle between the Greeks and the Persians.

In many religions, the main worship takes place indoors. However, Greek temples were not used in this way. Worshippers made their way up to the temple, and any sacrifices would take place at altars outside the temples. The inside of the temple housed the god or gods, which were normally represented by statues. The Parthenon was home to one of the largest statues of the ancient Greek world, a 40 foot (12 meter) tall statue of Athena made out of gold and ivory. This was placed in the *naos* (*NAH-ohs*), a rectangular room in the center of the temple. The naos did not have any windows and opened out onto a porch with columns. Some temples also had a second room off the back of the naos, which was used to store offerings that had been given to the gods. Other rooms might also have been used as treasuries, and these would have been fitted with strong doors.

The Influence of Greek Art

Greek civilization greatly influenced the world in many ways. During the period of the Renaissance (around 1450–1550), western artists rediscovered earlier forms of art and architecture from antiquity. Their imagination was caught by the beauty and skill that they found displayed in statues, pottery, temples, and monuments from ancient Greece. Some of the finest sculptors and artists (such as Canova and Michelangelo) were inspired to build on the work of the ancient Greeks and wished to produce works of similar beauty. The Italian architect Palladio was one of several to introduce classical architectural styles into Italy. From there, the new style spread throughout Europe to reach great popularity in the magnificent country houses and public buildings of eighteenth-century Britain and, later, the United States. This is why many civic buildings in towns and cities across the world, from London to Washington D.C., are recognizably classical in design.

Glossary

acanthus a flowering plant with spiky leaves, featured as a design on Corinthian columns

acropolis the fortified part of a city, built on high ground

agora marketplace

alabastron a tall, thin bottle, usually with a white background

amphora a storage pot, with a wide base and narrow neck

aryballos a small, squat jar, normally decorated

bouleterion council chamber

caryatid a female figure used to support part of a building

capital top of a column

centaur mythological creature, part human, part horse

Choes festival to mark the end of babyhood and the beginning of childhood

chous a small wine jug, used in Choes

corbeled a roof where each layer of the stone wall overlaps the layer beneath it

Corinthian type of column with an acanthus leaf design at the top

diadem a hair ornament

Doric type of column with a plain capital

dromos the stone pathway to the entrance of a tholos tomb

electrum metal, a mixture of gold and silver

fresco a wall painting

frieze a band of decoration around an object or building, such as a temple

funerary to do with funerals

gorgon a female monster with snakes for hair

gymnasium a sports ground

hydria a water pot

Ionic type of column with a volute, or swirl design, at the top

kantharos a two-handled drinking cup

kiln an oven used to fire pottery

kore a statue of a young woman, popular in the Archaic period

kouros a statue of a young man, popular in the Archaic period

krater a pot used to mix water and wine

kylix a drinking cup with a shallow, flat base

lapith a legendary race from ancient Greek myth

lekythos a pot made for burials, usually painted with pictures of mourners

loutrophoros a tall vase with long handles

mausoleum a large tomb named after the man who ordered it made, Mausolus

metope small sections on the outside of a temple, just below the roof

naos a rectangular room in the center of the temple

odeon indoor concert hall

oinochoe a jug for pouring wine

palaestra a building where wrestling took place

pediment one of two triangular spaces at each end of a roof

propylaea a grand entrance or stairway

pyxis a small circular box with a lid, used for makeup

satrap a local or provincial governor in the ancient Persian Empire

skyphos a drinking cup

sphinx a mythical creature with a lion's body and a woman's head

stoa a long rectangular building with walls at the back and sides

tholos a stone tomb with a domed roof

trident a three-pronged spear, such as that carried by Poseidon

triglyphs three carved upright bands separating one metope from the next

urn a vase, usually used for storage

volute swirl on the capital at the top of an Ionic column

votive item offered to fulfill a promise or vow as part of a religious ceremony

Glossary of Names

Achilles Greek hero in the Trojan War

Apollo god of the sun

Asclepius god of medicine

Athena goddess of war, arts and crafts, and wisdom; patron goddess of Athens

Biton a strong young man who died after sacrificing to the gods

Callimachus inventor of the Corinthian column design

Canova Venetian sculptor inspired by the art of classical Greece

Erechtheus a mythical king of Athens, attacked by Eumolpus

Eumolpus son of Poseidon, attacker of Athens

Hera goddess of childbirth, women, and marriage; wife of Zeus

Heracles demi-god; son of Zeus and Alcmene

Ictinus fifth-century architect who designed the Parthenon

Kleobis a strong young man who was commemorated with a large statue

Mausolus fourth-century satrap of a region of the Persian Empire

Medusa a beautiful gorgon who would turn to stone anyone who looked directly at her face

Michelangelo Italian painter, sculptor, poet, and architect influenced by classical Greek art

Nike goddess of victory

Palladio Italian architect who introduced classical Greek architectural styles to Italy

Pausanias a second-century C.E. travel writer

Penthesilea legendary queen of the Amazons, killed by Achilles

Pericles fifth-century leader of Athens

Pheidias fifth-century Athenian sculptor

Poseidon god of the sea, earthquakes, and horses; brother of Zeus and Hades

Themistocles an Athenian leader in the time of the Persian Wars

Zeus ruler of the gods; responsible for law, justice, and the protection of families; brother of Hades and Poseidon

Learn More About

Books

Ancient Greece (DK Eyewitness Books). New York: Dorling Kindersley, 2004.

Bentley, Diana. *The Seven Wonders of the Ancient World.* New York: Oxford University Press, 2001.

Biesty, Stephen. *Greece in Spectacular Cross Section.* Oxford: Oxford University Press, 2006.

Connolly, Peter and Hazel Dodge. *The Ancient City—Life in Classical Athens and Rome.* New York: Oxford University Press, 2000.

Hodge, Susie. *Art in History: Ancient Greek Art.* Des Plaines, Illinois: Heinemann Interactive Library, 1998.

Lassieur, Alison. *The Ancient Greeks* (People of the Ancient World). New York: Franklin Watts, 2004.

Malam, John and Mark Bergin. *An Ancient Greek Temple.* Columbus, Ohio: Peter Bedrick Books, 2001.

Mann, Elizabeth. *The Parthenon: The Height of Greek Civilization.* New York: Mikaya Press, 2006.

Ross, Stewart. *Ancient Greece—History in Stone.* San Diego, California: Silver Dolphin, 2002.

Spawforth, Tony. *The Complete Greek Temples.* New York: Thames and Hudson, 2006.

Web Sites

British Museum—Ancient Greece
www.ancient-greece.co.uk

Columbia University—Acropolis Virtual Tour
www.dkv.columbia.edu/vmc/learning/

Museums In Greece
www.ancient-greece.org/museum.html

HistoryWiz—For lovers of history
www.historywiz.com/anc-greece.htm

Metropolitan Museum of Art—Timeline of Art History
www.metmuseum.org/toah

National Archaeological Museum of Athens
www.culture.gr/2/21/214/21405m/
e21405m1.html

Olympia Museum
www.culture.gr/2/21/211/21107m/
e211gm04.html

TeacherOz—Greeks
www.teacheroz.com/greeks.html

The Classics Pages—Greek Art
www.users.globalnet.co.uk/~loxias/art.htm

ThinkQuest—Classical Greek Sculpture
http://library.thinkquest.org/23492/

University of Pennsylvania—The Ancient Greek World
www.museum.upenn.edu/Greek_World/
index.html

Voyage Back in Time—Ancient Greece and Rome
http://oncampus.richmond.edu/academics/
education/projects/webunits/greecerome/
index.html

World News Network—Ancient Greece
www.ancientgreece.com

Index